THE LITTLE DOOR SLIDES BACK

THE LITTLE DOOR SLIDES BACK

JEFF CLARK

FARRAR, STRAUS AND GIROUX

NEW YORK

Farrar, Straus and Giroux
19 Union Square West, New York 10003

Copyright © 1997 by Jeff Clark
Distributed in Canada by Douglas & McIntyre Ltd.
Printed in the United States of America
Originally published in 1997 by
Sun & Moon Press, Los Angeles
First Farrar, Straus and Giroux edition, 2004

Some of these works first appeared in *American Letters & Commentary*,
American Poetry Review, *The Baffler*, *Black Warrior Review*, *Boston Review*,
Flesh Dirt Forcefield, *Grand Street*, *Seneca Review*, *Volt*, *ZYZZYVA*, and
The Pushcart Prize XXII: Best of the Small Presses (Pushcart Press, 1997).

Library of Congress Cataloging-in-Publication Data
Clark, Jeff, 1971–
    The little door slides back / Jeff Clark.—
1st Farrar, Straus and Giroux ed.
        p. cm.
    ISBN 0-374-18858-0 (pbk. : alk. paper)
    I. Title

PS3603.L3645L58 2004
811'.6—dc22

                                    2003021115

www.fsgbooks.com

1 3 5 7 9 10 8 6 4 2

CONTENTS

THE LITTLE DOOR SLIDES BACK

LUNAR TERCETS

Things are not as we would have them be.
The moon is not a yellow sow
hung from a meat hook

on a drab shed wall: it is a moon.
Ashes do nothing
while we sleep: they are trees.

Satellites are not boys circling the low-back chairs
and record heaps of their drunken masters: they are machines.
The broad-hipped distended form stepping in the foam

is not someone going to wet her legs
but no one, phantom without live taxis.
She thinks, *Ships in the night are cruel ships.*

Even if, her left ear aimed at the brack
even if the claps and peeling lulled
she would not hear the canvas smack

there would be no din in the hull
no luminations in the masts:
tonight the moon soils its pallet

and what will emerge in the light by my bedside but No One,
her gown ratty from seawater and sand and from bedless cubicles
bedowned by whirling feathered things.

FUNESTE

If the smoke should go out
of my mouth and into
the jeweler's room,

if dawn should blue up now
his sash the plume goes through,
sucked out and upswooned,

if the jeweler's dawn
be fog-sodden or rued
by memory-beacons,

if I should write I down,
if I should now ruin
this dawn, return, he dies

MY INTERIOR

One bordello, three suites in the ass.
One two-bit nightery with chessboard in the back.
A snare drum, a pump, the rubble pile of a palace.
Siamese traps, and pink cocktail umbrellas
for the little blowsy ones who tramp the boulevards
and blue byways of my interior, tapping the asphalt

with their parasol-tips, unfurling their wings
to fly the Queen, tipping their fedoras to show their holes.
All day they pull cottons from inhalers that come down my conveyor.
But in my night, they bolt home and lock it tight, and move inward,
and begin to sniff by their basins, and whimper
We feel a first liquid now coming down the fuchsia

We hear Opal, we feel the bloodpump slow
Our lice awaken and slide to the wings
We nurse him with our holes, we love in his marrow
We snake out pipes, make rounds with caulk guns
Before dawn, debauched,
they try to stroke me to sleep in the bath . . .

High noontide in my interior: the red deer
wends out of my ravine when I wave, the gilled goat.
The shadows of my Frenchmen annihilate my little night-womps.
In my back-of-the-eyelid cinema: arabesques.
My best records are each hiss or moan or tremolo.
Your shadow annihilates my little day-womps.

Languor keeps my body from the desk.
Languor keeps the stockings on your legs.
Glare keeps the little ones at the conveyor
and out of the head . . . but then, from way off, with cranking
comes my night, and when it arrives
I go to it like a callboy to a C-note.

BLOW-NOTES

He said, "Take this gun," by the log house hearth, Babydoll
looped and blown on the log house love seat, her simper part
pixie, part slut, her breasts in situ, that is to say bare and
beaded with tiny brine gauds.

               She would be screwed now to that sofa by
him, who would afterward play something lento and maudlin
on the log house upright.

              "Stroke teeth" in the log house.

Make the ash box talk.

He said to me, "Take this gun and go to bed now."

                  And said,
"In the morning, when you wake and hear those shingle-pecks
and beeps, go out onto the deck and blow them down. Ten
dollars for each dust-to-dust and oil-to-oil woodpecker."

From a plastic sac, then arranged upon the earth:

white and blue

feathers.

Wet bits and bill.

At one a verdict from the log house:
a baleful low from Babydoll, and then from further

"Come, Love,

and bury the blue jays."

In my rotted missal, a Memorare:

Flared by white I fly to you, to you do I go, within you do I live, sphere to your orbit, around you do I heave, tide to your piling, despise not my wish, squid to my squall, to kill you, sinful and sorrowful, orbit to my sphere, despise not my want, Amen, until ends, to return you to fields, to return you to potential, O probable ending bed

Three a.m. was a mass
My pew a tawny
and shopworn sofa bed
        set up with animals and flowered sheets
his a red chair by a turntable

Home after a last set
        ruddy, not alive, beautiful clothes

                                Slurred canticles
Blow-matins
        Blow-lauds
                        One-ended antiphons
                                        Lines for an inward and
moonsick psalter.

We loved to walk then after a Host
or ride, was it a Cadillac?

        Ferries for certain

Sash flaps, bathroom door slams, and by my nose passes the bedroom's morning fragrance.

Of tombs and flu-sodden sailors his perfume, with a hint of wheat, and one of tobacco plumes above the bed

as my bed now, beware this, one of musk, two of wet cards, cuttlefish, pits

Confusion

In white pajamas in a hall of Salpêtrière: in a mantle of salt now, hanging in a coldroom.

In a poppy-blue drawing room: in a mantle of salt now, hanging in a coldroom.

In a stall: hanging in a coldroom.
In a field: in a coldroom.

Now movement in the room:

Whose kingdoms come

Confusion

On the intake the white birds alight

Where the branches collapse and expand

I went up in a lift and into a dressing room without a knock.
He was on a bed by a window, senseless,

                                        his mattress was a bale
of hay.

                                Flowing of a tap in the
bathroom, and in there Babydoll is stooped nude over the basin.

I took her hips and spun her around.
                                        Her tongue and lips were
green.
        She grinned and hopped her bottom onto the basin and
wrapped her legs around my waist, bits of blade in her teeth,
green spit on her breast

Confusion

The glauzy and noisome Soul-Siphon settles like a brume.

Soul-Siphon settles like ash spat from a dust devil, floating into and cooming a thicket.

Soul-Siphon settles on a pigeon's-blood smoking jacket and cessed hair of one pouring rum on a piano lid, who is going to light it and begin the next number.

Soul-Siphon cooms a lounge, then hole hotel

Confusion

In the spleen-slapped humid gloom two want
to embrace and so
arise in their room

Con

Two wanted to

embrace and so

arose

ST. NEMELE

Who hovers above me now,
in a black coat, the table lit
as if by a tenebrist?
Whose mane glints
as if slicked
with pomade not pitch?

Who isn't tincture of pine
but of pall and cyst.
Whose eyes are holes
not spangles in a hall.
Nemele, I wander around
embracing waists of trees

who won't speak,
who don't attend to atonalities.
When I lied after noon
like the one half of a brothel pair,
you opened your gown
and in there

in bleary stills
I saw an anvil,
then a
then an unwell
—what?—in an evil antedawn.
In the evening you opened your gown—

Nemele, you must have gone.
Why now phantoms, why now gauze,
green fins, dead swans?
Why someone in a yellow dusk
with piece outslung
at one end of Pont-Neuf?

Have you gone
darkward, or where
the white mare—

Who hovers above me now
pricks in manifold forms

ON AN IRON COT

The way it was decorated, one might have thought the trailer vacant, or that its tenant were tasteless and poor. But the boy had not time in which to consult the antique merchants of the city, nor was he interested in art. I cannot say, despite months of meticulous surveillance, that he fancied anything besides sleep, nakedness, and cigarettes.

Nor did he fancy his occupation, since not a single moment of my patronage of the circus did his grin while playing the ukulele or riding his tiny bicycle seem anything but counterfeit. He had a tenuous rapport with the ringmaster, who many nights, after the show had ended, would burst through the boy's door and denounce his religious tippling. "Little man," he would curse, "I have in mind to replace you with a chimpanzee if you insist on poisoning yourself like this each night. And this chimp can play the theremin like a virtuoso!"

Ruined, sweet boy . . . When at last I had the courage to reveal to him my infatuation, I entered his trailer, at the hour I assumed he would be in the ring, to deposit a love letter for him. To author, it had required several hours, so many amorous sweeps of the pen, that twice I had to

I won't ever forgive myself for failing to observe the clearly rendered announcement, hung early in the day:

NOON SHOW CANCELED
NEXT SHOW 7:30 P.M.

When I unlocked the back door of the boy's trailer with a file, and moved into the kitchen to place the letter on his table, a whiff of oil arrested my pulse, and my beloved boy, thinking I were a thief, sprang upon me and knocked me unconscious with a bottle.

When I came to, some form, my letter in its hand, was humping itself with laughter, and on an iron cot a sickly dog with its ears back and its tail slapping the sheet.

NAPOLEONETTE

I had a small part in *Napoleonette*. I wrapped some meat in newsprint and handed it to a woman. The scene was shot in one morning. Since I am not a fan of film, I went home, and in the afternoon the phone rang me from sleep. Geschenk was angry, he said, "All it was was the lady reaching over the counter—for *nothing!*—you weren't even *there!*"

Sometimes a ghost entered my heart and I could feel, and sometimes phrases entered my mind and I could speak, with reason. But never was I able to stay a man long enough to remain him.

INVAGINATIONS

I passed the afternoon wandering the bazaar, lingering in stalls so long I almost abandoned my plans in order to shop.

There was a hall tree I wanted badly, a cracked klieg light, a picture book, a suede armchair in which I fell asleep and was therefore escorted out of a shop cellar and up into wet night.

I was famished and had some pho, and tipped the waiter poorly, for seating me near the toilets.

Then it was fully time and I hustled toward the building, my brow pimpled with sweat and pomade, the revolver plucking hairs from my belly.

Outside I fidgeted endlessly with my coat buttons, and had such a fit of cussing that when I caught the doorman mid-leer his lips were apart.

I paid and went through the hot parlor and into the hall, which rumbled with the roars of drunks.

Lucienne was up in the fore, beside a piano. Someone cranked a gramophone and aimed its horn at her.

The pianist straightened and began the first tinklings of "Parlez-Moi d'Amour" . . .

I was rapt in the middle of the floor, the cellist pushing down his bow, Lucienne singing now, but it was so unlike what I had wanted, her voice so like the whine of a looped supplicant, the strings so like eunuchs bawling in a larder, the shouts in the bar lifting not ceasing, grease all over my fingers, she was so unlike for whom I had yearned, so thin and blemished, her eyes like wood nickels, brows penciled on, and it occurred to me then that her aspect was nearly identical with one of those auraless derelicts in velour and corduroy, in yellow alley-light, a terrible blush in the cheeks, unzipping her duffel in the snow, having a long look into a compact, squatting down, hand on the third or fourth step of some back stoop, to release that steam so unlike exhalations, her white ass so terrifying.

One "spell" is followed almost immediately by the next, so that he has no time to reflect, or to compose himself. Here he is a "palmist," here suddenly an "assassin." If he is not sending me out of his room and away from his transports, he is calling me back in to say, *Would you believe I am now*— I rarely respond to his pleas, since I don't know which to believe. The cats run away from him. He thinks he heard someone call him "daft" this afternoon as the doors of an elevator were closing. When he goes to the bathroom to shave and to wash, he growls about ———

Tonight bed drives him mad. His "acts are divined there," and he becomes agitated when he ought to sleep. The woman in the next apartment is working furiously toward the floor with someone in the next apartment. He makes too much of their noise, and if I call to him from the sofa in the living room he rants. Bed drives him *especially mad*. He says he loathes sleep, it is like a "vertiginous womb." I lock him in. I hear him curse and wonder what is commandeering him now.

He was sweet and wanted affection. He stood within the door and whined. He begged that I caress him, that I fondle and hold him. But I refused. After one kiss, in which he gripped my hair and pulled my mouth to his own, I refused—

And even when his is no one and demands nothing I refuse now. He tugs at my arms and if I slap him he quiets meekly. Himself, he often will attempt to console me with platitudes: *For a brief moment I abandoned you . . .*

Tonight he calls himself a "nympholept."

"Mass of odorous catatonia."

"You drew up my lids: there was a pained mouth there. Pulled down the lids: the mouth laughed!"

Tonight he wails in the tub like a child—

"Shave it!"

"I will *wade* into the Pacific and kiss my mother!"

This evening he was "blind," so that I was able to approach and watch him. He plaited strands of copper wire into a grotesque brooch of filigree, then, sniffing the air, dropped it, and chanted

New deck, black and white, several high, shuffled at night   *new deck*
New deck, white and black, six to a stack, words on the back   *new deck*

This evening he was "small," so that I was able to approach and hold him in my arms. He filled a green pipe and held it to my lips . . .

This morning he was "foam balls," so that I was able to approach and gather him up and stuff him into my camera bag and take him to the ocean . . . but there he became a sea horse while I swam and squirmed from his towel down the sand and into the water.

MARIE-PRISTINE

FOR HOOPY

There is about three minutes that I received from you this postal card of eleven lines—but a silence of *three years*? I had fears to write you—*fears*—imagining your address to be empty, or your body.

Have you this month received a large cake with twenty-three candles, as your pen told me once it is custom there?

Yes, I see that you did get an auto. Pray, get now an airplane, that you may undertake a journey to me, to know my new person.

Have you found yet the picture of my city, of poor relief? And the plan of my country, is it clear where I am to be found? (I will go on waiting impatiently for the reliefs promised by your letter of three years past, so if you can speedily, I have desires to see your new face.)

Winter-days are gone. I go in the meadow now to no end, whereas I was passing all the days at my window, a blanket in my shoulder-tops, watching in the morning the boulevard events, at noontime the seamen row from the mud berth, in the evening the pimp on the walk, who casts and who reels back, it is typical, nothing. But the brougham of this man! Have you there a word for this auto, for its great length and luster? "Pimp-sedan"? Or simply "limousine"? Does it grow red as a noisette in your thinking, the wonderment at how such a one as a pimp—a mack!—should be permitted to stain my staring around, not to say my nights, my town . . . ah, but he is ever there. His name is Larousse.

Now the gibbering of his associates in the late night is such that I must close my window, and stifle.

Forgetfulness! Take up once more the envelope that bore this to you. It is so: half my name, known by you so many years, is gone from me. It was simple and the death of two birds: my head turns no more to the oft-called "Marie-Christine," and more, I delight my familiars with this fancy-exotic.

"Who, these familiars?"

—the feathered, you remember them. (And my dictionary says that I am Mary-Pure for you now?)

Do you remember my bath songs, how they disturbed you? The hi-fi reminds me.

I have now an old stereoscope. Do you know the one? Also three stereotypes: the plaza of my city; a campanile, the bell of whom will make illusions of to and fro when the device is jostled; and the sea-coast. Do you often see it? Or is this perchance no longer a predilection? I have reveries of it there, so dark and chill to the feet, the wood portions (the sea-sticks) across the sand, and the wind who pushed the cypress trees backward.

Your desire: without camera I can no more snare my image than send it to you. But if you must have me, I will tell you how to see: a gauze over the eyes, the vigor going from the hair, the breast unfirms, a tooth here and there is dark.

And! my fright when at first the telephone rings.

Also have me rushing down the stair for the mails that seldom arrive.

Will you believe that I now write, in this same hand, my more vital prayers? Especially this: "Take the Devil from my within." I place them on this table and sleep then, whereas all my life, you remember from your nights here, I was going to bed, putting out the lamp, and then making my prayers there. For me now, dialogue becomes a fright.

I am slapped, and downtrod, in so many moments by Him, and here has become another common prayer: "Let me be," or, "Today I beg one furlough from your gall." Is it by bêtises and false airs I have deserved His slaps in the night? Or do you too get them? Am I an abecedarian in my suffering? Though: if you would accompany me once in my night, you would see my felonies, and would not blame Him his bruisings. But please, do not have me as a pity-wanting anchorite, knelt in the fogbow by his feet. Rather, have me in the human way: one part fear, one devotion.

(A terror to wonder: do the slaps come from the other way?)

Where does it go now, your life? Is it according to your desires, and content? When this arrives at your box, and after, into your hand, receive from me one embrace, and see me now as not so different from what memory you guard. And then, to be gracious, I will summon you to my beach, for a picnic, and then will see that the Ocean closes, for I will have waited all day!

Pray, more postal cards with lines of you. Even: navigate by wine this very night to your writing-desk. In this wish I kiss your cheek, and wave most tenderly.

SOME INFORMATION ABOUT TWENTY-THREE YEARS OF EXISTENCE

AFTER MICHAUX

1970

In the shrift, she says, "It is *always* moving, even in slumber, never still. It is *always* quivering. Too much liquor, Father, and I fear the womb will get murky, and the little one, when it emerges, will already be a sot."

Pressed, at the coast (the breakers), by the crapulous mass, its talking like a boat turning over. Tepid sac that night, powdery floes. Taxied through rumblechambers.

1971

Terror in the birthing room: the little door slides back—

First mews were of pissulence, not want.

In the depot Deliriope.

1972

Antler-nubs cropped, tail docked.

Taken, in the morning, out of my box and into their fetid room.
His hands would then be rubbed.

Thrown into the sea.

Begin inward composition of *Aphorisms of Legless*.

Considering: what will be my first utterance?

1973

First utterance: "Horse horse whose horse?"

Second utterance: "Mal dedans."

First compositions for musical saw.

1974

Wondering: *Pre-dawn? Preyed on? Prie-dieu?*

Mother says, "*Please* come—and bring a pick."

Oil.

Beginning to understand pine trees.

1979

Meditations on Melody and Transparency.

Plug, untree, mourn my first beast.

1980

Tended by Francis in rear of Yeoman's Lounge, Anaheim Sheraton.

Fathoming his pomade.

Who was Francis?

Homemade birthday card from Auntie, in which is calligraphed:

The idiot knows the wear of his soles can be traced to two or three boulevards in particular . . .

. . . and can't stop walking them!

Her gift: an antediluvian grammar book. Discover that, in "Subjects for Themes," she has marked, "Of What Use Are Flowers?" "Street Arabs," "Sailors," "Pluck," "An Old-Fashioned Cornhusking," "Affectation and Naturalness," "Was the Execution of Jay Unjust?"

Twirling.

1982

Model homes. Kisses from a decorator named Dots.

Impregnated by an alien duneflower.

Autodialogues begin.

1983

First ejaculation—accidental—: into a bottle of bath salts.

Entranced and mortified by crepuscular birdclatter.

Parable of the Hangared Satellite.

April: receiving, as if in earphones, someone else's thinking.

1984

My impressions are dim impressions. I console myself thus: "My impressions are merely *not of this dimension*."

—Alas, they are of this dimension, and are like corduroy in a palace cloakroom.

Ruptures.

Sometimes a small wind on the back of the neck.

All notions occur to me beginning, "If I were . . ."

Swaying outside make-out closets.

There is no grid in the desert.

Joy from a robe pocket.

1988

First Skoal fiasco.

Introduced to a breast: daunted.

August: far away, cannot move anyone with my body.

Yellow paw.

Speech at Elks Lodge: "Thank you, ladies and gentlemen, for the generous scholarship. Now there will be a cleft in the linoleum, and between sash-openings and -closings of flame, you'll see me descend."

Saying to the boys, in the circle, "Boys—aren't we starting to loathe
line breaks like

> 'What a fine thing it was to walk that Autumn out of one's
> Body and in-
> To a death fil-
> Led
> With ether-booms and no more
> Am-
> Ber horse-dust-
> Ed vials'?"

Blame the Church for my being an emulator.

Writes Auntie, *All I ask is that you show me pictures, that you play your records when I have been delivered from the night to your stoop mangled, my pant legs torn.*

Excommunicated by Nature.

Waving goodbye to a billow of smoke from a mortuary chimney.

Drawn from my sidewalk into a fashionable party. Standing among six or seven who discuss film. Am a kind of would-be participant, eating cheese, occasionally nodding. Someone turning to me, asking, "What do you think of So-and-So?"

"I don't know about that . . . but I've read *Mrs. Dallow.*"

Parable of the Hangared Satellite. The choice was given it to depart its hangar and enter the firmament, or to rest immobile inside it, alone with the wicked technician.

Identical dreams: muzzled mouth, queer chandelier.

1992

In depot P, prying open lockers, looking into bags.

Imitations of Immortality.

Wondering: seaweed or eel?

Around the neck a noose? Collapsed halo?

1993

Sounds like altos in a deep end.

Encounter first of several scenarios of or including images of trapped birds.

Quixotism.

Novantiquities.

Sidling to the organ: threnodies.

Remembering how one faded into a last Polaroid,
and took a last kiss—before an aurora he and I
heard horns in the harbor—him whose
pleas now leave me.

1995

Passed out . . . fell forward into the Royal. Struck some letters with my face: h, m.

Why have I developed no personal logorhythms?

Terror now in the shrift: the little—

Terror now in the Hangar: the little door slides back:

GAUCHE MARE

"O hear!"

But what may I hear, Dear Lost, if you are mute to me? I knew by several of my own deaths that you would not always be there with your pen, and that to merely write toward the ghost of you is enough . . . but if you do hold me now, let me kiss you with this:

Are you alive?

"O hear!"

But who could ease my rack with his own hands strapped?

Or your Tight Apple is rotten—anyway it . . . this shall be the last!

In other times, my Lost, when you were evil, I wrote in your book, "Why are you cruelest to whom you most adore?" If you have departed by your own hand, how, I think, if earth has finished for you would I hear you? If a ghost you would be now by your ocean, I know, in your cypress tree where we entered upward and watched the breakers. And the asses of . . . mothers—

Or fog? Didn't fog have a tongue for these ears? It most certainly did. The two of us had then—as I recall—actual affection for one another, and for Night White rolling in . . . spitting . . . actual potions that propelled us up howeverso much . . . or down, submerged in seedy pool. Now it appears to my nose and rathermore NERVE one of us has grown an immense hole . . . a hole . . .

Steps to the cavern. His figure doubles. Cleans it with a swab. You were never at Choate, were you? Neither were you Sorbonne nor any

Institute . . . you were briefly nighttime turd in a Desert diaper, briefly a plum in a Valley's pocket . . . how then explain your airs?

What voices I hear now are not loved by me at all, so that I have you speak at my tableside the words you were wont to write once from your first separate city:

"Your kisses, on paper, are like snow-sown poppy seeds."

"Marshal your thoughts . . ."

I saw in the dark bay here little yellow lamps—impervious to my reason, as were those small stars of which constellation we did not know:

"From the fisheries of Haifa: Majnoon's Balls."

Pray, if I came soon to you again, is there yet time to pick up the salt-foam in your hands and blow it away, in the dark as you did then, where it was lighted for a moment by a tiniest moon?

Do you still see this: we went through a vapor at daybreak to a church and were chided by the Father with a woman's voice: "Daffodils *wilt.*"

There is no treat in our box now, no souvenirs of our ocean, no sea-stairs or minor dunes, no frondacious lines.

I abandoned your wrath in I do not know what state, in whirly rain—do you know that a certain loamstink in the heart of my park calls back that day? You said to the Father, "Do you suppose that I will *always* have her nose inside my Oeil de Gabès?" and after, at break-

fast, you said to the waiter, "Coffee for myself, and a glass of death . . .
for my cousin . . . The Gauche Mare."

And I: "And a pile, please, of spunk for my cousin Ass."

—"A snare a snare is little Gauche Mare

Out of her trap comes sulfurous air

Her saddle is sodden, and worn besides

The Ranger's awaying to other rides."

"Tom and snare are siblings."

—"His mother laid heron traps throughout the desert—"

"Station Agents, we are looking for a lost item, a brown leather
holster containing . . . half a wand."

—"A head is vibrating."

Station Agents, we are looking for a lost item

DEMONOLOGUE

It was fascinating to induce   fear
I was proceeding with   how shall I say it

With recorder out and buttons depressed
When he raised in the windowlight

His face Lord over hers
When I raised his face and held it there

DEMONOLOGUE

I know his scent and infest there
Would like to lie in him one more hour

Mix of meats in wraps of sullied cotton
Blood and plugged blood

In the windowlight

He invites anything to his face
All night from his mouth

Whiny arraignments, mendications

And devestation   when without strength
Invitations are ignored

DEMONOLOGUE

I had a ward I adored and tortured in four ways

I mocked his wish to be rid of me

I made it impossible for him to sit still

I was   how shall I say it   Proprietor

Of his parts Lord   I was Lassitude

He was like a horse to me I locked him in then and starved him
As for my horse Lord I starved him and introduced ticks to his body

It was dark inside all day except when at noon and three and six
It was dark inside save when at noon three and six I opened the door
It was only lit when I opened the door and showed him an apple

And yet I believe I thought now and then I loved my horse Lord

Thus the more barbarous my treatment the less his visage and voice
The more barbarous my acts the less his face and thought disturbed
The more the horse moaned the less I was inclined to Lord the *less*

THE FOILY INCH

Who follows one to the park

Who's behind one all the way

Whose scent is cat's ass and fed breath
blown down past one's head
by breeze that in one's mind is Wind

Whose refrain behind one on the walk
is drowned by wild parrots

DAIM-COQS

Howling daim-coqs fill the rows
Herons from wires love hooves in hose

And now backstage the oils you know
And now backstage

And backstage what was slack arose
And backstage lungs in floating does
And backstage who speaks false explodes
And backstage thighs to strokings go
And backstage overflows the bowels
And backstage tongue and lips lave toes
And backstage foam on glowing throats

Strings

                    blood in forms in throes

The felt hammers

DEMONOLOGUE

This morning from his bed Lord
I led him to Flesh Ornaments

This morning from his bed Lord
I led him to a Pink Gamepiece Manufacture

This morning in his bed Lord
I hummed him   old Hopi numbers

This morning in his bed Lord
I gave him an orange plastic crab that honks

This morning in his bed
was ended by an engine

This morning in his bed
I lent him wire   Kill the Pilot!
          Saturated headwater   dark red floating bills
                    red slicks

A glance at the radar: they're there

In his bed   a pang to remember

I am dead and Brother knows
Beneath the grass that Brother mows

In his bed   a pang to remember
    my first bit of milk
        in a desert

Joy from a robe pocket

In his bed
      cursing female cathedral   chlorophyll   immense will
          one I never touched   never shall

Great pain   to recall   a sage rooming house
    I loved when a mosquito

Lime cologne when a servant

In his bed
    legs when drops in a Mojave pool

He wakes   and as he moves   a switch is
    typically toggled   that is all?

Then no more: I confess in their bed   No one
        has sent me
            No one deploys

Only pool   only fly   one cell
        in left cheek of servant

In his bed
never again to smuggle in   personal vials
        Never again Liar   never to be
            mucus in a merchant marine   never
a thousand dollars in a wallet

This minute I can rest in bed as a part
        can have brown eyes   heavy brow
can hear, can breathe
                        —What's this?

11:11   My last act?   My last
        Please!   shall be an oath
            please   *A beautiful record*
        11:
A beautiful record will never be destroyed

MALIBATUS

When he came down from the hills, a crowd surrounded him, from which a girl advanced and knelt before him, and said, "If you are willing, you can make me clean." He stooped and caressed her face. "I am willing," he said. "Be clean."

But the girl was not altered. He touched her again: she shivered but did not heal.

Then the mob resumed its welter. Several wrapped their arms around him and cried; one wailed, "I am dying . . ."

The girl thrust her way from the group and ran home. When she passed swearing through her door, he was there, at the table.

"Since I cannot cleanse you, I wish to employ you." He swept his arm across the tabletop, and there appeared a pad of paper, a bottle of ink, and a pen. Beckoning the objects, he said, "With these you will record what you see, and it will be holy," and was gone.

The girl moved to—

Gusts. With screeching, as of gulls burning.

Such chaos in her stomach that vomit—

Slurred song issued then from her wet lips and then, dispossessed of the command of her body, thoughtless and without sense, her own hand was pouring the ink down her throat, unfamiliar ambiences were quickly tainting the landscape out the window, her own legs were hurtling her out the door and through the yard. Tumescent, eyes rolled back, her own legs were hurtling her toward the well.

SLAGNOTES

In this lode of bulblight
    whose hand strokes my elbow

from whose throat, *Go to bed, night is possessed by shadow*
    Its ware is waste, nothing worthwhile is open now

Who pulls bows
    across the teeth of lunate saws?

After the devolution of midnight
    in this lode of bulblight

who lists past my cell
    scattering slagnotes pell-mell?

MAL DE DUSK

Who deals in scales and fleshrecord players
Who wafts in the imbroglio of scents
Whose siblings are spilled in musty drawers
Whose oil fouls the linens whose down and lint

We'll stay hidden behind the folding screen
We'll watch through the slit the splayed and white knees
And mouth of whose ablutions and libating
Make dusk din and make dusk ping and make dusk

IF I DON'T RETURN

If I don't return it's because on the way I was drawn from my sidewalk into Tswun-hwa's lobby, or else because a morose and robotic young man pulled me by the lapels of my coat into a doorway and demanded, "What is meant by this *word*?" But before I could reply, someone stepped between us and said, "Say, for example, I give you a little lamp, out of which you rub a genie . . . who then offers you a wish. We would expect you to *wish* for something, but you would instead try to *confuse* him, you might insist he change himself into a shaft, a patio, you know, or one of those musical greeting cards, or you might say to him, 'In my canoe I am pelted by leshies,' or, 'Il y a de temps en temps un riant rouge con qui me visite dans ma nuit et qui s'appele Monsieur D. Able—' We've all been given a musical greeting card, haven't we? Hallmark made one that was white with brown flecks and played 'Knees on Carpet—'"

That is when a small pony from the Track Homes shoved her aside and made a loud noise with its lips and cried, "Please . . . you must wish for nothing but a small FARM and then TAKE ME THERE and then KILL ME."

TETHERED COUPLETS

Your mother walks oddly
your father knows Iran,

you make love to a certain hand, open a cherished book,
wish to approach the zone in which monodies—

Thus the maudlin albums,
worn though ever cherished

a certain stang in the throat, slow intakes
and exhalations, hammerings

In the day what remains
are blacks on the face, stains on the hands

What vanishes is the image of a certain visage
is the image of a certain gray flank

are the dead words and notes from the throats of this
certain plainting fathom feared and not imagined

THE GHOST HAS NO HOME

This morning in an alleyway I was startled by a face
I seemed to recognize, in a dormer above a garage
and so slunk up to him, who was ranting quietly,
mauling the mind of some imagined ear out the pane
as if maligned, or high, like one
moony and almost witless in a poppy ditch,
or one waking ill and supine
in a wet bed of opening mullein:
"I have no desire to theorize language—
I was raised modestly and have sinned unspeakably.
I would rather waylay and destroy
whose voice molests me."
On his desk a thin book I knew, a tragedy
whose residue was a Sentry's couplet I half-knew
and began to recite—startling him who turning was outwardly
unknown to me—, " 'Does it hurt in your ears—' "
"Fuck Antigone—I detest language, I *detest* artifice,
I would rather waylay and molest
the beast that has imagined and pent me here."

SEA, SWALLOW ME

This morning in an alleyway you were startled by a face
in a dormer above a white, vine-groped garage.
I shall not appear
when my form has been erased
concealed like that in your inward scenery.
I'll return rather as would the ghost of an oceanic scent
in prairie air. I'll touch you briefly—
I swear to neither hurt nor lure you.
Let me touch you briefly, then destroy me, for I assure you . . .

THE GHOST HAS NO HOME

This morning in a dormer I was startled by a face
subterraneously white and walking with such a gait
down the pavement that when I cleared the pane
of breath—

        Behind me a muzziness then hissed:

"Together we shall name Fear   'Benign Cyst'
then I shall be deceased, you shall be missed"

              Together we dismantled its nest

SHE WILL DESTROY YOU

It is alleged in my temple that mine
has arrived. In my neck it is alleged.
Your horrid book I adored this morning
alleges this minute mine has arrived,
stellar, with fog careening . . . frauds of moon.
In the crack and in the port: starry.
In the legs' A, the A's eggs it is alleged.
By abandoned prose, a nightlong tic,
either eye knows it has arrived, astrose, and loathed—
She smoked through pleas by the bougainvillea.
Something flashed in a distant apartment.
Love so occurs to me, and Mine, and though
I'm allowed no line to surround it, Affrightment.

CLISTHERET

I heard a sleave of song
   from an upper window
and moved in the sun to find them—
I wanted to call to them
   beg them to lean out,
and go on

But there was no window
   I was on sand,
their lullaby came from the waves,
there were no waves,
   but a glinting derelict named—no derelict named
Delirious Iris, I am home, there is snow

from a filmy coal-blue sky, mechanical
   hissing, great heat, green clouds in the bath—please,
An eye in the lives of my loves
A lung in the lives of my loves
   and the two things You keep . . . keys:
to liberty, to manacle

DRINKING BEACH

Where have you gone
my shrinking beach

where is your kelp
that held me under
until I grew slumbrous

where is your froth
your brine
that filled my lungs
my lost beach
who obliged to help
destroy me should
inward gongs
announce Now the red
vacant arcade
will be thronged
with the loud gulls
of longing

where have you gone
my banging waves
sobbed wind

in which I would lie
and speak aloud
to one detected as now
beneath the sand

one who too
has known and been
seduced by you
reduced in this
desert to aqualonging

my shrinking beach I fear
would not again
if I waded in
and swam way out
caress me sandward
my beach who
because I have left you
will ingest me deeply
when I enter you again
my pined for, should I ever near you again
my pined for and dreamt of
my drinking beach

LA PLUS BELLE STROPHE
DE ROBERT DESNOS

FROM "RROSE SELAVY"

44. Amorous traveler of tender maps, why nourish your nights
    with tarts of ash?

SWEET TO FIENDS

The worst of kinds of my chameleon:
sweet to this one, sweet to that, sweet to fiends

Loathing them only internally,
loathing loathing, loath to autoalter

REFRAIN FROM TRANSPORTS

BLUDGEON YOUR FANCIES

More than bluebells and dolorous roams
Attract me through these woods   do tonight
Rearward unrhapsodic
Sounds slap me forward
Hellbehindedly
Along a fogsloppy
Lunatinged flight of loam—

Yards away, although I cannot measure—
Outraged by their keepers' out-of-kennel taunts,
Unpent a pair of hounds
Rail in trail, stanged by scent

Though I esteem my skin sanitized,
Having been pleasantly still here in the
One hour between late bath and this
Undoing of later atmospheres of ephedrine.
Gaseous keepers,
Hazy forms moss-hung from high panes in psychic solariums:
That you still be so shrewd as to delude we
Sick with cliché with thoughts of the sound of
    "pursuit by hounds . . ."

THE GRASS

Oriented in new tropics, away from bong
and poles, no nightholes forced in horse
folly, searching then in vein for direction,
now you are out in the grass, the sun severe,
if you please, "the blades" at your neck so dear,
all stirs to learn, the cock that fills for the skyward grove
is far finer to goad upon bent blades in noon's garment

than to retie down in night's robe—Movement,
going, I love to arrive, to move . . .
whoever They are are near me then quickly not near.
To take the hand, to send it out, or to sever,
yes, to sever the screen that keeps me mute to my affection,
to go down and avow, with mouth at affection's sixth source,
Minatory mornings none where I've gone.

TERCETS

Clatter in the landscape,
                  sick refrain,
                                    third suck, third sigh, third—

Fabricator and Inseminator of each dirge, soul's imprimatur,
thaumaturge of cane and snow and metronome,

                                        wont so often

to harry one to the verge of slurring,

is that you, that ragging half-bird
                                    at the malmade and maltuned
organ, is that yours, that bawling as if from a stuck cock?

Clatter in the landscape,
                        sick refrain,
                                    third suck, third sigh, third
scrape,

after you or I have ended this apprenticeship,

will I have derived

a more cunning way of slurring?

But is that you that clatter in the landscape,
                              is that you that sick
refrain,
        third suck, third sigh, third crank,

or is it spirits sprung from bone's tank?

                                    Is it spirit's tongue,
or one of your bitter dead birds',

                        twine around its bill all day,

pisted through dirt to lakes

                        where your minions spit, and in

thickets, the other birds'—

Clamorous sigher in the landscape,

                                              while others have linnets

that alight, will feed

Tomorrow, in night, in three warm cores,

I'll prepare

(Sentries mount guard.)

GEORG TRAKL